The Wandering Albatross

Written by Marilyn Woolley
Series Consultant: Linda Hoyt

WorldWise™
Content-based Learning

Contents

Chapter 1	Fantastic flying feats	4
	Why is this bird fantastic?	6
Chapter 2	Where does the wandering albatross live?	8
	The south polar region	9
	The Southern Ocean	10
Chapter 3	How does the wandering albatross survive?	12
	Using the wind	12
	Body structure and features	14
Chapter 4	Nesting and breeding	20
	Nests and eggs	21
	The takeoff	22
	The landing	22
	Feeding the hungry chick	23
	The young adult	23
Chapter 5	The wandering albatross at risk	24
	Longline fishing	26
Chapter 6	Protecting the wandering albatross	28
Conclusion		30
Glossary		31
Index		32

Chapter 1

Fantastic flying feats

In the days of sailing ships, when journeys across the ocean were long, dangerous and lonely, sometimes a wandering albatross would fly near a ship for several days, never landing on the water – always flying. Some sailors thought that it was a sign of good luck – that it would protect their ship from harm. Others thought it was a bad sign or that someone was about to die. But it was agreed that to kill an albatross would cause a curse to fall upon the entire crew.

The albatross was always a sight of wonder and mystery.

Over the years it has also been a mystery to many scientists. They have wondered how this very large bird can make a journey of 16,000 kilometres without stopping and **circumnavigate** the earth in 46 days.

How does this bird stay in the air for such long periods of time? How can it stay away from land for so long?

Did you know?

There are 22 **species** of albatross. It is nicknamed the "lord of the sky". This is because an albatross can stay in the sky for hours without flapping its wings. As it glides, it turns to soar up in the sky and then soars down to skim the tips of the waves.

5

Why is this bird fantastic?

How fast can it fly?

The wandering albatross can fly at speeds of up to 90 kilometres per hour. It can fly for days on end at an average speed of almost 30 kilometres per hour.

How far can it fly?

The wandering albatross can make a single flying journey of 16,000 kilometres over the roughest ocean on Earth. It can cover over 1,000 kilometres each day to gather food and bring it back to its nest.

How did the wandering albatross get its name?

The scientist Carl Linnaeus gave this bird its scientific name *Diomedea exulans* in 1758. Its name translates to "wandering bird" because of its flying feats over the ocean.

How big is the wandering albatross?

The wandering albatross is one of the largest birds on Earth. Its body can be up to 1.4 metres long, and it weighs about 11 kilograms. Its wingspan, at up to 3.6 metres, is the longest among all birds.

Try this

Stand against a wall. Stretch out your arms. Ask a friend to measure your arm span. Now measure 3.6 metres. Compare your arm span to the wingspan of a wandering albatross.

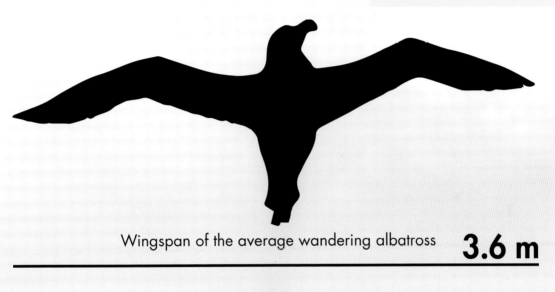

Wingspan of the average wandering albatross **3.6 m**

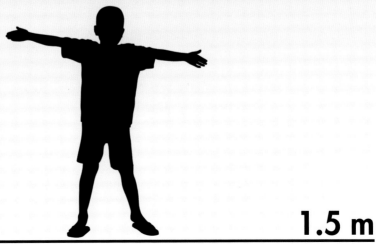

1.5 m

Arm span of the average 11-year-old boy

7

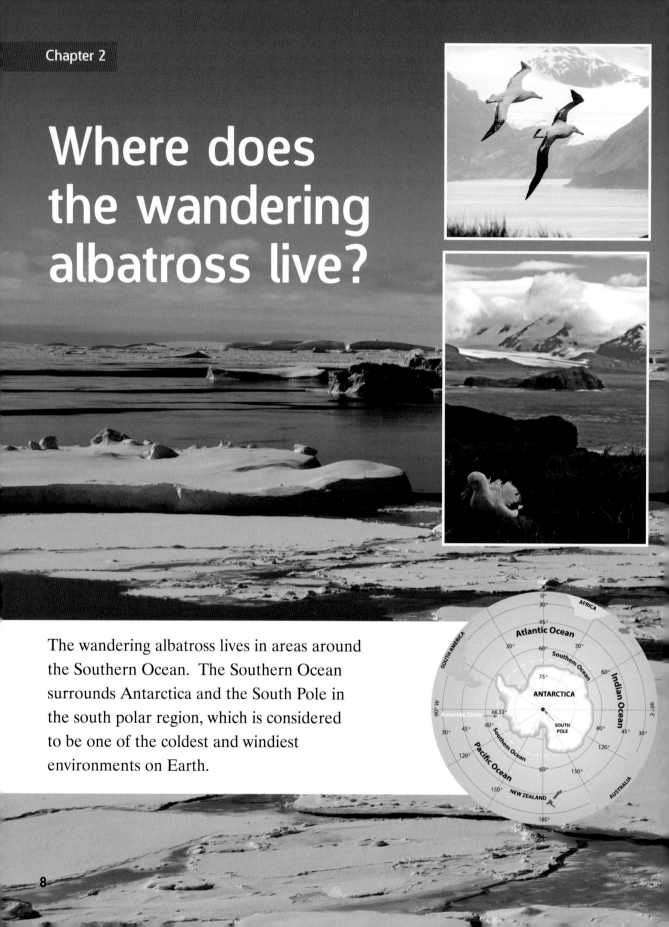

Chapter 2

Where does the wandering albatross live?

The wandering albatross lives in areas around the Southern Ocean. The Southern Ocean surrounds Antarctica and the South Pole in the south polar region, which is considered to be one of the coldest and windiest environments on Earth.

The south polar region

The area around the South Pole is far colder than the area around the North Pole. Antarctica is made up of an ice cap that is about 300 metres thick. It is larger than Europe, the United States and Mexico combined.

Antarctica is also the highest continent on Earth – three times higher than any other continent. It contains massive snow-covered mountains, many of which rise straight from the sea. **Glaciers** cut through these mountains and send icebergs crashing into the water.

The permanent ice cap reflects about 85 per cent of the sun's rays into space, which means this polar region has the brightest reflected sunlight, but very little warmth.

 Did you know?

The average annual temperature in the south polar region ranges from −10° Celsius to −60° Celsius. This region has very long cold winters of complete darkness. During this time, much of the Southern Ocean freezes over and most animals and birds escape north to warmer regions.

The Southern Ocean

The air over the Southern Ocean is very cold. Cold air rushes down the sides of the high Antarctic mountains, causing ferocious winds of over 290 kilometres per hour. These westerly winds are the strongest on Earth and more powerful than those in a hurricane. They whip the ocean into swirling, choppy foam and cause spray to rise from waves that are up to 20 metres high. The Southern Ocean is the roughest ocean on Earth. And yet it is home to the wandering albatross.

Think about ...

Think about how high 20-metre waves are. How many storeys are in a building as high as 20 metres?

Icy waters of the Southern Ocean

Chapter 3

How does the wandering albatross survive?

The wandering albatross's way of flying and its body structure and features enable it to survive.

Using the wind

The bird uses the strong winds just above the high waves in the Southern Ocean as a source of energy to help its movement. It faces into the wind with its long wings outstretched at right angles to its body. Its wings generate enough lift to enable the bird to turn and travel at an angle to the force of the wind.

As it travels over the water, the albatross uses the wind that is **deflected** upwards as it blows across the waves. The bird makes a zigzag movement across the face of the wind from one wave to another. This repetitive up-and-down movement enables it to glide in the air for hours without beating its wings. This means that it uses very little energy. The bird can stay airborne with minimum effort and can keep flying without needing to come ashore to rest.

? **Did you know?**

Engineers have studied the wandering albatross to try to **decode** its flight secrets.

Tracking the wandering albatross's flying technique

To find out more about the bird's flying technique, a team of scientists attached GPS trackers to 20 wandering albatrosses. These trackers allowed them to measure each bird's position every ten seconds during their flight path and to record how the bird soars without a single flap of its wings.

1 First, the bird climbs into the wind and when it is up high, it curves away from the wind.

2 Then it makes a swooping descent at speeds of up to almost 145 kilometres per hour.

3 When it is close to the surface of the waves, it curves away from the wind again.

Tracking where and how far wandering albatrosses travel

Scientists attach small radio transmitters to the backs of the birds to gather evidence of how far and where they fly. The transmitters send regular signals to **satellites** high in the sky. The signals come back to a receiving station on Earth. Scientists can measure the distance and location of each flight.

Body structure and features

Bones

The bones of a wandering albatross are very light but strong.
They make up only 20 per cent of its body weight. The wandering
albatross has special **tendons** in its chest muscles that lock its long
wings into an open extended position when gliding. These tendons
allow it to make small changes to the position of its wings during
flight. Unlike most other birds, it does not have to constantly flap
its wings to stay up in the air.

Wings

The wandering albatross has long pointed wings. Its wing feathers slide over one another so that the surface of the wings remains smooth and the air flows easily over them. These features improve the bird's ability to move through the air because it has a **streamlined** shape. As it glides using the wind, the length and surface area of the spread-out wings are big enough to prevent the albatross from falling.

The wandering albatross has a strong beak and tubular nostrils.

Beak

The shape and features of the bird's beak and nostrils allow it to find food quickly in the ocean. It has a long, strong, and sharp hooked beak that can catch food moving on the surface of the water. The wandering albatross is also able to **filter** nutrients from the seawater with its beak. Its tubed nostrils allow the bird to get rid of excess salt from the seawater.

Find out more

Find out how much a wandering albatross can eat at one time. How much would this food weigh?

Wandering albatross sitting on the water to feed

Digestion

The wandering albatross can eat up to one-third of its body weight at one feeding session. It has an acidic stomach that breaks down food, and it can digest food quickly. This food changes into an oily substance that acts like a type of fuel to give the bird more energy for its long flights.

Did you know?

The wandering albatross has a strong sense of smell and is able to smell food from a long distance. It can follow this scent line along the top of the waves.

17

Feathers

The Southern Ocean is a harsh and windy place. But occasionally there is no wind. During these times, the wandering albatross sits on the water for hours at a time. It keeps its feathers waterproof by spreading oil over them from a gland in the skin at the base of its tail. During the night, it gorges on squid, krill, or the flesh of dead penguins or seals that float on the surface of the water.

To take off from its sitting position, the albatross runs across the top of the waves, using its large webbed feet as paddles to propel itself into the air.

Did you know?
Sometimes the wandering albatross eats too much food and is unable to fly.

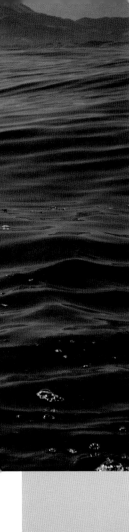

Air sacs and body clock

As it flies, the wandering albatross breathes in oxygen that travels into air sacs and the lungs. The bird has many different air sacs where air is stored and then used as needed throughout its long flight.

The bird has great powers of navigation. It can keep on its flight path because it has an inbuilt map of landforms and stars. It **instinctively** knows where to fly and for how long.

After ten years, the wandering albatross knows that it is time to come back to the island where it hatched to breed and raise its own young.

Chapter 4

Nesting and breeding

The wandering albatross breeds on subantarctic islands between the latitudes of 46 degrees and 56 degrees south. These islands include South Georgia, Macquarie, Kerguelen, and the Prince Edward Islands. Every two years, in November, wandering albatrosses return to one of these islands. After mating, the birds make their nests on the western, **windward** side of the island. Pairs of wandering albatrosses mate for life.

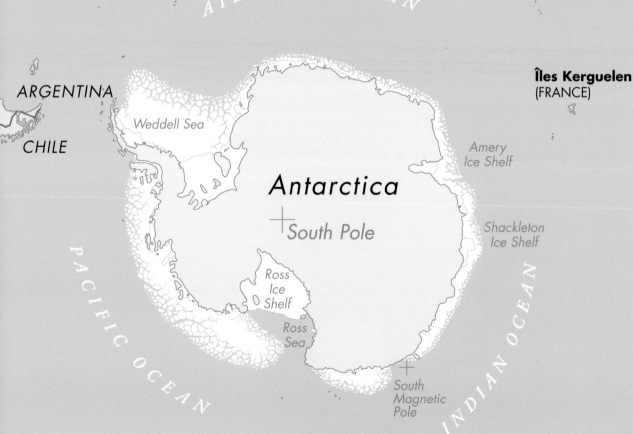

South Georgia Islands
(UNITED KINGDOM)

Prince Edward Islands
(SOUTH AFRICA)

ATLANTIC OCEAN

ARGENTINA

CHILE

Weddell Sea

Îles Kerguelen
(FRANCE)

Amery
Ice Shelf

Antarctica

+ South Pole

Shackleton
Ice Shelf

PACIFIC OCEAN

Ross
Ice
Shelf

Ross
Sea

South
Magnetic
Pole

INDIAN OCEAN

Macquarie Island
(AUSTRALIA)

Nests and eggs

The adult pair makes a mud nest in tussock grass or ferns near exposed cliffs or ridges. The nest is shaped like a curved bowl that is one metre wide at the base and half a metre wide at the top. The female lays a single egg in a hollow area in the top of the nest. She lays the egg between December and March, which is the warmest time of the year in this very cold environment. This large egg can weigh up to 500 grams (half a kilogram).

The parents take turns sitting on the nest to **incubate** the egg. It takes 79 days for the egg to hatch. While one is sitting, the other goes out to sea to hunt for food to eat and bring back.

Try this

Study the size of a hen's egg. Find out how much bigger and heavier the egg of a wandering albatross is compared to a hen's egg. What other birds lay a large egg like this?

The takeoff

When a wandering albatross leaves its nest, it has to create an air current to lift up its body. It uses a long runway along a path through the grass, similar to those that aeroplanes use in takeoff. Stamping on the ground with its large webbed feet, the bird runs into the wind coming towards it. This is known as the prevailing wind or headwind. It beats its wings to increase the speed of the air passing over them. These movements give the bird enough lift to rise off the ground.

The landing

When a wandering albatross returns to the nest, it lands on the same runway that it took off from. While still in the air, it lowers the tail section of its body, puts it feet out in front as air brakes, and then starts paddling with its feet. It makes a type of crash landing and tips forward onto its chest, before struggling up and staggering along to its nest.

Feeding the hungry chick

The chick hatches during the cold, dark winter months. The parents feed it every few days. It takes them more than a year to raise their chick. The chick grows to weigh 12 kilograms, which is one kilogram heavier than its parents. Both adults then hunt for food and visit the chick at times to provide food. In the nest during the dark months, the chick learns the star and moon maps in the sky, as well as the position of the sun during the day as summer approaches. This information will help it navigate on its future flying journeys. It also observes its surroundings to make a visual map of what to look for when it returns to this same place to breed.

The chick's brown **down feathers** change to full feathers in about 270 days. When this happens, it is a young adult ready to learn to fly and live in the ocean.

The young adult

Birds learn to fly by both practice and memory. The young adult wandering albatross runs and flaps its wings to make them stronger over many days before it finally takes off out to sea. It then begins its life flying around the Southern Ocean. Unfortunately, many young adults do not survive their **arduous** sea journeys.

Chapter 5

The wandering albatross at risk

The wandering albatross is quite well protected by its **remote** location and can live for up to 60 years. Even though it has few natural predators at sea, some birds do not survive the harsh conditions of the south polar region. The greatest threat to its survival is posed by humans.

Wandering albatrosses breed on only a few islands. People have explored, visited or worked on some of these islands, and brought animal pests such as rats and reindeer with them. Rats have eaten the wandering albatrosses' eggs from the nests on the ground. Reindeer have trampled the tussock grass and nests and destroyed the eggs.

Each year, about 6,000 people visit South Georgia Island, including tourists, yacht crews, science and weather researchers, and maintenance workers. Even though there are strict regulations about where people can visit, accidental damage can be done to the nests.

But it is in the open ocean where wandering albatrosses are most at risk from people. They die in large numbers because they follow longline fishing boats. They are looking for food and get caught on baited fishing hooks.

Longline fishing

Longline fishing began in the waters of the Southern Ocean in the 1950s. In this method of fishing, a series of baited, hooked fishing lines are laid out at intervals along a long main line like tree branches, and then reeled out to sea from the back of fishing vessels. These longlines of up to 100 metres have small weights attached to make them sink just under the surface of the water. The lines can carry hundreds or even thousands of baited hooks and can be either anchored or left drifting on the water.

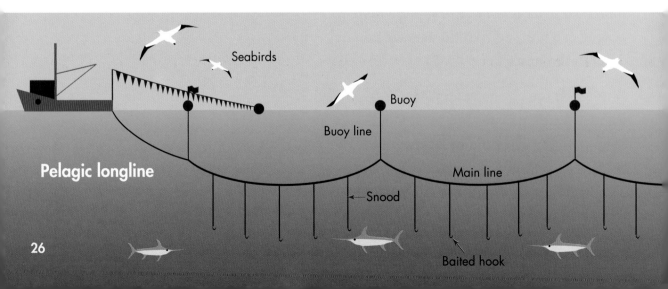

Seabirds

Buoy

Buoy line

Pelagic longline

Main line

Snood

Baited hook

As the lines are being set into the water or hauled back into the ship, the bait on the hooks is visible to wandering albatrosses. Because these birds have keen eyesight and a strong sense of smell, they dive towards the bait and swallow both it and the hook and then become entangled in the lines. They are then known as seabird bycatch. The weighted line drags the birds beneath the water and they drown.

It is estimated that between 50 and 100 million hooks are set each year in the Southern Ocean, and tens of thousands of birds are killed. Scientists have estimated that one albatross is killed every five minutes by fishing vessels. As a result, the numbers of wandering albatrosses are continuing to decline. On the IUCN Red List of Threatened Species they are classified as being vulnerable to becoming extinct.

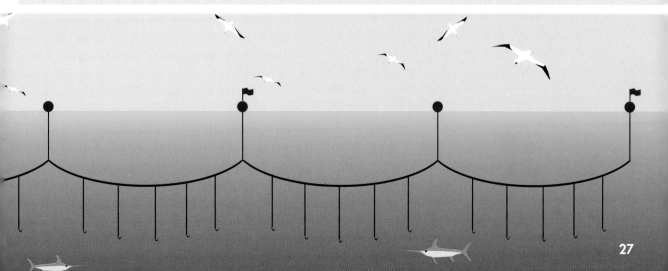

Chapter 6

Protecting the wandering albatross

Regulations have been set to protect the wandering albatross and reduce the number of deaths at sea.

International agreements attempt to protect albatrosses and reduce bycatch from longline fishing. These include the Agreement on the Conservation of Albatrosses and Petrels, and the Convention for the Conservation of Antarctic Marine Living Resources.

Technology used on fishing vessels today helps reduce the number of birds that drown on longline hooks. Fisherpeople on ships must take steps to reduce the number of birds taken as bycatch.

Techniques are being tested to determine which are the most effective in preventing wandering albatross deaths.

In addition, some waters are closed to fishing when wandering albatrosses are breeding on nearby islands and foraging in the sea for food. But the Southern Ocean is a vast space, and it is very hard to **monitor** the activities of all fishing vessels.

Fisherpeople need to:

- put heavier weights on the line or use machines to make them sink more quickly
- use bird-scaring materials or devices such as coloured streamers over the area where the hooks enter the water
- modify the fishing hooks so that it's harder for the birds to take them
- set lines at night to reduce the visibility of the bait
- keep discarded fish or waste on board when setting or hauling in the lines
- thaw the bait before putting it out to sea because frozen baits float longer on the surface

Conclusion

The wandering albatross is one of the most studied birds on Earth. This is because of its size, its features and its amazing soaring flight patterns in the coldest and windiest environment on the planet. Scientists continue to be puzzled by its behaviour, and there is still a great deal of research to be done.

Sadly, the number of wandering albatrosses is declining each year. If people do not work harder to protect them these magnificent birds may be extinct by the end of this century.

Glossary

arduous	difficult or tiring
circumnavigate	to travel all the way around something
decode	to interpret language or behaviour
deflected	changed direction
down feathers	soft, fluffy feathers that cover a young bird
filter	to remove unwanted material
glaciers	slow-moving masses or rivers of ice
incubate	to keep eggs warm and bring them to the hatching stage
instinctively	to naturally know how to do something
monitor	to keep track of
remote	isolated
satellites	spacecraft that collect information
species	a group of animals or plants that are very similar
streamlined	to have a smooth shape that moves easily through air or water
tendons	strong tissues that connect muscle to bone
windward	facing the wind

Index

Antarctica 8, 9

bycatch 27, 28, 29

circumnavigate 5, 31

Europe 9

feathers 15, 18, 23, 31

glaciers 9, 31

ice cap   9

Kerguelen Islands 20

Linnaeus, Carl 6

longline fishing 25, 26–27, 28

Macquarie Island 20

Mexico 9

North Pole 9

Prince Edward Islands 20

radio transmitters 13

reindeer 25

South Georgia Island 20, 25

south polar region 8, 9, 24

South Pole 8, 9

Southern Ocean 8, 9, 10, 11, 12, 18, 23, 26, 27, 29

tracking 13

United States 9

wind 8, 10, 12, 13, 15, 18, 20, 22, 23, 30